CHUR
FROM THE
INSIDE

LAURA TRENEER

BRF

The Bible Reading Fellowship
15 The Chambers, Vineyard
Abingdon OX14 3FE
brf.org.uk

The Bible Reading Fellowship (BRF) is a Registered Charity (233280)

ISBN 978 0 85746 554 2
First published 2017
10 9 8 7 6 5 4 3 2 1 0
All rights reserved

Acknowledgements
Scripture quotations are taken from The Holy Bible, New
International Version (Anglicised edition) copyright © 1979, 1984,
2011 by Biblica. Used by permission of Hodder & Stoughton
Publishers, an Hachette UK company. All rights reserved. 'NIV' is a
registered trademark of Biblica. UK trademark number 1448790

Every effort has been made to trace and contact copyright owners
for material used in this resource. We apologise for any inadvertent
omissions or errors, and would ask those concerned to contact us
so that full acknowledgement can be made in the future.

A catalogue record for this book is available from the British Library

Printed and bound in the UK by Zenith Media NP4 0DQ

Contents

Introduction   4

1. Why it matters   7

2. What to consider first   17

  What is our current reality?   17

  What is our core message?   20

  Who is our focus?   32

  Are we communicating a cohesive, consistent,
       credible identity?   38

  Are our expectations realistic and shared?   39

3. Essential next steps   41

  Choose your tool—15 in detail   42

  Choose your look   70

  Plan your year   72

  Plan your content   75

  Find your team   77

4. Toolkit   81

Notes   92

Introduction

This series of books starts with the understanding that it is primarily and ultimately God who communicates. He's equipped us to take part. If it seems our resources are limited, our time, our capacity, the hope is that these books will show you tools you didn't realise you had, and ways to put them to use. They're best when they're used together, so although the focus here is how we communicate inside the building, this needs to be integrated with how we communicate before people step inside, and digitally, wherever people are all week.

Have you ever seen the programme *Come Dine with Me*? People open up their homes to strangers and try to impress them with their dinner party 'entertaining'. The concept of opening our homes to strangers can be a novelty in British culture, although perhaps less so, we hope, to churchgoers. I met someone recently who asked me 'What does your husband do?' 'Actually he's a church minister.' 'Wow… um, so I guess you must do lots of entertaining? How many people do you reckon you have round in an average week?' My honest answer was more people than she'd had round in a year. She was astonished. But we'd never describe it as 'entertaining'—just simple hospitality, of the 'help yourself to a cuppa, grab a chair, I'm all ears' variety. It's not flash. We never serve starters.

Is there a risk sometimes that churches, in an effort to be welcoming, offer 'entertaining' rather than hospitality when strangers enter our doors? Do we invite people primarily in the hope that they'll notice and comment on how welcoming we are, or are we focused on offering the kind of occasionally thankless 'hospitality… without grumbling' the Bible speaks of in 1 Peter 4:9? Henri Nouwen describes hospitality as:

the creation of free space where the stranger can enter and become a friend instead of an enemy. Hospitality is not to change people, but to offer them space where change can take place. It is not to bring men and women over to our side, but to offer freedom not disturbed by dividing lines.[1]

Your church building, or the physical space where you meet, does not belong to you. It has been provided by God as a place that is open to anyone. What is communicated inside to those who enter— intentionally or not—will always be far broader than anything we can control. There is freedom for us in this. The failures and successes of our communication may well be unseen. Opening our churches is an intentional act of hospitality. If this offers the 'space where change can take place', as Nouwen suggests, the changes will be mediated primarily by the Holy Spirit.

Churches have an immense opportunity! Not only do they get to be places of sacramental worship, teaching, communion, fellowship and all those other things that are understood by most UK Christians, though not necessarily by their neighbours. They also get to be lights in their community, changing perceptions of Jesus Christ. Churches get to ask the big questions in the public sphere.

This series is for those who feel responsibility for church communications, and for those who think they make a difference. There is plenty that churches can use from the marketing world, from free resources online and from other churches. The options can seem overwhelming—but time, budget and, let's face it, imagination, can be limited. I hope the tools in these books will help you form a simple strategy and plan that starts squarely in the reality of your situation. It's written so that the intimidated can relax and the goal-oriented can focus.

1

Why it matters

I know why it matters, you say! Why on earth would I be reading a book on church communication otherwise? But you'll need to justify to others why you want to make improvements. Here are three of the many reasons to put in the effort.

Crossing the threshold is a big deal

Where would be unfamiliar territory for you? Places you forget exist, perhaps. A bookies for some, a primary school for others. A nightclub. A gym. A snooker club. A casino. A youth club.

Revd Dr Sandra Millar tells the story of going to McDonalds with a friend, both in dog collars:

Both of us began by saying, 'It's years since I have been in here.' Strange memories of taking the children lurked, or even further back to student days. But recently? I have lost touch. Not my world any more. It made me think how hard it is to come into church. We know what it is about and what everything is for.

We know the menu, the procedure, the practice. But those who come back with memories feel awkward and uncomfortable. Sometimes they want something that echoes the memory, sometimes they just need a friendly smile.[2]

Churches can be in this middle ground for people, not entirely foreign, but not familiar either, whiffing not of hamburgers but of reminiscence. The doors in many churches seem to have been built for giants, rock-rimmed and grand. Even the many churches meeting in school buildings have connotations for visitors, as school isn't a positive experience for everyone. The memories confront them the minute the door is open. As Don Draper says in the TV series *Mad Men*: 'Nostalgia—it's delicate... but potent. It literally means, "the pain from an old wound". It's a twinge in your heart, far more powerful than memory alone.'[3]

If you are on your own, don't know anyone or, even worse, haven't been invited, then crossing the threshold is a Very Big Deal. Or, if you are desperate for church and for God, but are wary of Christians, it can be even harder. This is why churches who are serious about welcome know that it begins before people enter the door—ideally with an invitation and a person. They also become sensitive to everything that might exacerbate a potentially tricky encounter.

I work with web designers who talk about eliminating 'user anxiety' (when we don't know what to do next) and 'friction' (when what ought to be smooth is not). Entering church can be fraught with friction (why am I being given these books and papers?) and user anxiety (where should I sit?). A church that is aware of these things can address them.

Many megachurches in the US employ people full-time to consider their church communication. One describes her job like this:

Your church has a message. A message of truth, hope and purpose. But before people in your community encounter that message, they encounter your church. Your job is to maximize the things that attract people to the message and remove the things that repel them.[4]

No church sets out to be unwelcoming. We just forget. We forget that when we welcome a stranger we enact a gospel of reconciliation. It demonstrates that we are in the world, but not of it, loving others as Christ loves us. Again and again Jesus disregarded social norms to reach out to those he noticed, whether or not he knew their names. Actually in the gospels those he reaches are often nameless to us. Nameless, but known and remembered.

All the research confirms that it is loving relationships that keep people in church. It's what Jesus told us to do: love one another! This means not ignoring people. This means 'crossing the room', as evangelist Bill Hybels has emphasised, as a reciprocal action to someone's crossing the threshold.

Look at a visitor's body language. If it's not attempting to create an invisibility cloak you could say something as simple as 'Hi, I don't think we've met before—my name's Laura', or 'Hello, looks like you've just arrived, can I get you a cup of tea?' Easy words, easier with practice. Then, and this is hugely important, remember their name next time, and the time after, and introduce them to others.

People don't want friendly churches. They want churches where they can make friends.

You may have heard the mantra 'Belong believe behave'. Churches so often accidentally reverse this, and insist through their own behaviour and culture that people first behave ('Do as we do!'); then, if newcomers believe, they can finally belong. 'Belong' first means proving the statement found on one of the most popular posters from Christian Publishing and Outreach (CPO), where I work: 'Wherever you're from, wherever you're going, you're welcome here.'

Communication isn't just verbal

You may have come across the VARK model of learning styles, or ways we absorb information: Visual, Auditory (through hearing), Read/write and Kinaesthetic (through experience and movement). Which is most prevalent in your church?

Improving communication inside the church matters because it acknowledges we are multisensory, and makes the most of this. Visual communication in churches goes beyond posters and boards. It's the state of the floor, the size of the building, the colours, the paint, the facial expressions. It's the font on the screen as well as the font for baptisms. It's the stained glass, the candles, the clip art, the cross.

Jesus told stories with words, but it was the pictures he created that stirred the imagination. The father running to the prodigal son. The farmer clambering for the lost sheep. Visual communication is how we think. It's how we feel. It's how we remember.

And yet the church communicates in an overwhelmingly auditory way. We sing. We preach. There is more about this later, but it's worth pointing out that there are 250,000 deaf people in the UK. Chapter 4 lists some of those seeking to reach them. In our communication let's not neglect disabilities and special needs of different kinds.

People in churches are disproportionately university-educated compared to the general population. We rely on communication through the written word—and yet one in six UK adults has a reading age lower than an eleven-year-old.[5]

Kinaesthetically, we learn about a church through the comfort (or not) of the seating, the rituals around where we go for coffee, the smells, the warmth (or not). 'Where do I go? Will I knock something over? I don't fit in. It smells strange. I've never been anywhere like this before.' I was moved by the true story in the 'Everybody Welcome' course of the lady who was moved to tears when someone shook her hand as she entered church. It turns out it was her first human touch in three years.

Customer service professionals say it takes anything from seven to twelve positive experiences to make up for one unresolved negative experience. A positive church experience may be healing hurts from the past. We are all different, and all our senses need to be engaged.

Improvements enhance and equip in ways you may not expect

Some will say that a church needs to change internal attitudes before worrying about its external communication. I disagree. Change the appearance and you can begin to change the heart. There are few easier ways to make an immediate impact on a church than a physical makeover. It raises expectations, boosts morale and mobilises volunteers. As one pastor wrote, after a creative missions team significantly improved the church's visual communications in just a week: 'It has lifted a huge weight off my shoulders. It enables us to focus more.'[6]

When you improve communication and think about your visual identity, it requires thinking about who you are as a community, and joining the visual dots between who you are inside the building, outside, and online. The effect is all-encompassing.

This book suggests incremental changes that will have a disproportionate effect on a congregation, equipping them for outreach and encouraging them to invite their friends. Recommendations from friends continually comes out in research as the most effective 'advertising'. Improved communications create a positive story of change. Make it a story worth talking about. The consequences of failure when we experiment are actually very low... but if they touch a nerve, spark an interest or use a new talent, the potential is enormous. Don't let perfectionism stifle creativity. Have a go.

The National Churches Trust found that nearly a third of UK Anglican churches don't have a toilet.[7] As one BBC mockumentary commented, 'The people weren't in church because the Wi-Fi was better at Starbucks.' These are not peripheral barriers. They're also not insurmountable. Chapter 4 lists sources of help, many of them free. For those that aren't, consider including communications as part of the budget for outreach rather than administration. This is core to the church's mission! As the Archbishop of Canterbury, Justin Welby, has said, the church budget is 'theology in figures'.[8] If you can't create a fit-for-purpose church kitchen, you can still practise hospitality with some flasks or cafetières. Conversations are free. Thought is free. Articulating values, assessing what you're saying with the perspective of an 'outsider', social media: these do not cost money. Where you find practical barriers you'll also find a handy cliché to combat them: where there's a will there's a way.

The summary of why it matters

The National Churches Trust have found that 86% of the UK population have been in a church at some point in the last year.[9] When we communicate as a church, in action, in truth, it is an act of love. The biblical phrase 'hospitality without grumbling' was mentioned earlier. Now consider that in the context of the scripture passage as a whole:

The end of all things is near. Therefore be alert and of sober mind so that you may pray. Above all, love each other deeply, because love covers over a multitude of sins. Offer hospitality to one another without grumbling. Each of you should use whatever gift you have received to serve others, as faithful stewards of God's grace in its various forms. If anyone speaks, they should do so as one who speaks the very words of God. If anyone serves, they should do so with the strength God provides, so that in all things God may be praised through Jesus Christ.[10]

If God provides the strength, God provides the gifts and provides the words. If love indeed covers over a multitude of sins and the end is near, whatever that may look like, what excuse do we have for not moving beyond complacency and inertia to love in action?

2

What to consider first

Before you set out to grapple with all the ways you communicate outside the church, there are five strategic questions that can form the foundation of a long-term plan. Ideally discuss these with a group.

1. What is our current reality?
2. What is our core message?
3. Who is our focus?
4. Are we communicating a cohesive, consistent, credible identity?
5. Are our expectations realistic and shared?

1. What is our current reality?

These exercises, hopefully as a group, will help you see your church communications with fresh eyes and create ideas which might work in your context.

A learning and listening walkabout

Essential for any church leader at any stage. Give searching attention to activities you'd forgotten happened or never visited, what is and isn't communicated, and on a Sunday, how people consume and respond to the information they're given. Do people actually read the news-sheet? Who looks at the noticeboard? What are the communications which happen just from the inertia of long-ingrained rhythms (the tyranny of the weekly, monthly or annual), and which show evidence of creative flourish and one-off experimentation? You may need to be aware of 'insider syndrome', where overfamiliarity creates selective blindness. Someone new and searingly honest could be helpful.

A pile of your printed communication

Does it look like it's from one place? Is the information consistent? Does each piece reflect well on you and on the rest of the pile? Looking at the whole rather than the individual parts exposes the places that jar, and the places that set the bar. It's only by doing this that you'll get the true picture. Be aware of 'ritualised slightly rubbishness', where stuff that isn't good is there only because it's always been there.

The 'in or out' test

By now you'll probably have a target list for upgrades. You'll know what has the potential for improvement.

Try to place them on a sliding scale, from 100% outward-facing (a leaflet for newcomers) to entirely internal (the flower rota). Can you make your 'in' more 'out'? Is the balance of 'out' to 'in' as you'd want it? Here's another test: survey the congregation to find out whether they actually use the magazine, weekly handout, website, text reminders and noticeboard. If it's for them and they're not really using it, could your resources be better focused outward?

What does it take for change?

Steve Aisthorpe in *The Invisible Church* writes this:

A precept of the 16th century reformation translates as 'the church reformed and always being reformed'. We need to be agile, learning, and relearning what it means to be faithful to the unchanging Christ in a context that is always in flux. Flexibility is a vital element of [a] healthy church. Church leaders need to foster a culture where 'always being reformed' is the norm.[11]

If you do what you've always done you'll get what you've always got. Modelling a willingness for change actually mobilises others to change too. If churches don't want to concern themselves with change, they certainly don't need to worry about the future.

'But Mike will kill me if I change the…!' I hear you cry. The fear of upsetting people in church can come from genuine pastoral care. At other times it's just fear, and we know what the Bible says about that. Sometimes the relationship trumps the review, but I've worked with Mike, and others like him. He's not as intransigent as you assume. If the vision is clear, the support is available, possibly an alternative role offered, you may find that your stumbling block is his millstone, and together the path can be cleared.

2. What is our core message?

Start-up companies talk about developing an 'elevator pitch': the three sentences or fewer that you could recite off by heart in the time it takes to 'ride the elevator', summarising who you are, what you do and why you do it. The church equivalent might be the mission statement, the vision statement or the strapline. If you know your core message as a church it can act as a centrifugal force on the rest of your communications. In terms of strategy this is the message in shining lights at the centre. The rest should sit somewhere in its glow.

Typical Sunday morning service. Song has finished. Souls warming up. Up to the microphone. 'And now a few notices…' The notices are the battleground of what Kevin Hendricks calls 'the gospel vs. housekeeping'.[12] They're the crucible in which the really key stuff in church life ('Your friends may not know the true Christmas story. We're telling it at carols on the 18th at 6.30 pm. Invite them!') gets lost in the detail ('If you're in the bell-ringing group that meets on the second Wednesday of the month, you need to pick up your new rota from Pete and Sue').

When you know your core message you can point to it, rather than distracting with irrelevant detail that confuses visitors. The battle can even disappear altogether, so that the most mundane of housekeeping information actually points to the gospel, or at least doesn't distract from it.

Some churches give new life to notices and announcements by asking children to give them, or using video, or props. Some limit them to the facts only and to those that are relevant to everyone. As Kem Meyer puts it in a book on church communication aptly called *Less Chaos. Less Noise*, 'the more events you promote, the less important each becomes. The more announcements, the less people hear. The more handouts, the harder it is for people to find what they're looking for.'[13]

Ask this: 'Why do we do this thing we're talking about?' If someone can answer that question on stage, ideally with a story, it will be elevated from a notice to a testimony. Instead of asking for volunteers for the parent and toddler group, ask someone who helps to say what they get out of serving God in that way, or even better, someone who attends to say what a difference it makes to them.

Try finishing these sentences:

- We're putting effort into this event because…
- We're doing this again, because last time this is what happened…
- This information matters because…
- The story behind this group is…
- If you want to know what difference it makes, here's someone's story…

Stories get repeated. Facts get read. Stories can be exciting. Facts can be boring. Worse—it can set a precedent for more boring information in the future.

You will have your own instinctive methods of prioritising your communication and creating a hierarchy. Here's an example of a tool from Chuck Scoggins from Church Marketing Sucks (a blog to help churches with their communications):[14]

	Relevant to many	Relevant to few
Big potential impact	**A**	**B**
Small potential impact	**C**	**D**

Communications Tool	A	B	C	D
Stage announcement	X			
Promo video	X			
Email	X			
Text notification	X			
Brochure/flyer	X	X		
Sign-up table	X	X	X	
Social mention	X	X	X	X
Website	X	X	X	X

Core values shared by many churches, absolutely in no particular order, are:

- prayer
- world mission/international

- children and young people
- welcoming locals
- welcoming one-time visitors
- historical heritage
- social justice
- the centrality of the gospel

Here are examples of how other churches have communicated these core values. This list is not exhaustive. Use it as a starter for your own ideas.

Prayer

- If you have people available to pray for others, make them identifiable with lanyards or badges.
- One church used a bubble machine as an alternative to incense. As the bubbles floated, all ages were invited to pop them as an act of prayer first for friends, then for countries, then for themselves.
- Invite people to sign up for regular emails with a prayer calendar for the week or month.
- Talk about prayer in your posters and welcome. 'Open for prayer' is an invitation to come in and pray, but also a challenge—are you open?
- One church asked CPO to produce banners for the inside of churches saying 'This is the prayer place. Prayer and pastoral care here for you.'

- 24-7 prayer have excellent ideas for creative 'prayer spaces' within a church, which don't need to be restricted to a special event, and could be used all year round. You will also find ideas from the 'Thy Kingdom Come' prayer initiative and from Messy Church.[15]

World mission/international

- Flags in the building say, 'We are international, or if we're not, we'd like to be.' Plus they're colourful.
- A map, ideally a Peters Projection world map, keeps horizons broad and vision large. Surely no one can take offence at a map. We are part of a worldwide church. Good to remember.
- CPO have customisable posters, banners and postcards saying 'Welcome' (and others saying 'Happy Christmas') in many languages.
- Missionary boards or tables do not need to feature out-of-date letters and curling magazines. If you have a missions board, keep it simple, current, educational and prayer-focused. Give material to those who'll use it. Then—and believe me, this will help—make friends with the shredder and recycling bin for all the unnecessary old paper.

Children and young people

- Visible toys, games and activities and an area with comfortable flooring communicate welcome even where there's no group for children. Children and those looking after them may well end up on the floor whether there are chairs or not.
- If you're one of the thousands of churches offering parent and toddler groups, make sure the church know about it, with pictures or stories (but no photos of children without permission).
- Think 'school classroom display' and cover a wall or board with something colourful and interactive, involving all ages. Examples CPO offer include trees with leaves to stick on, hands with handprints, feet with footsteps, and palm leaves. These communicate that 'children are a crucial part of our family here, just as important as the adults'. And always involve children in the service when you can, as an integral part.

Stacks of ideas are available from Messy Church, www. youthandchildrens.work and others. Bob Jackson writes that 'the church with many children is likely to project health and joy, to flourish and grow. The childless church faces a dreary inevitable demise. So the children are the Church's most crucial members.'[16]

The need for excellent work with young people is urgent. A 2016 study showed that only half of churches regularly discussed basic Christian beliefs with young people.[17] Another study showed that parents are failing to share their faith with their children as much as we might expect.[18] The Head of Research at Youthscape wrote this in 2016:

When I feel anxious about the young people in our small church youth group and question whether our efforts are making any difference, I remember that our God multiplied the young boy's lunch—two fish and five loaves—into enough food to feed thousands. If we keep bringing the small offering that we can manage, God will be faithful to multiply.[19]

Welcoming locals

- The 'Everybody Welcome Course' has three aims: to help individuals have a welcoming approach, to identify priorities for change, and to set up a welcome team. Welcome badges with names are a great place to start. One Catholic parish for their 'Year of Welcome' put together a great list of ideas for discussion to kick things off.[20]
- Some churches use local maps in a display linked to prayer, with a prayer plan for different streets.

- Some churches make a conscious effort to communicate what goes on during the week. If you do this using photos rather than words, try to make the photos inclusive. We all look for photos of me, of someone I know, a friend of someone I know, and failing that, someone I can imagine knowing, someone like me. If there's none of those we won't look for long. Similarly, if everyone standing up to speak is of the same gender, skin colour, age and (whisper it) class, we can communicate exclusion, cliques or worse— even if that would never be our intention. Seeing ourselves as others see us can be uncomfortable.

Welcoming one-time visitors

- Clear directions to toilets, exits and halls are the least we'd expect in a cinema, gym or community centre. Churches should be as reassuringly simple as everywhere else. See the advice on page 54.
- There are useful suggestions online for some very specific categories of one-off visitors: for those coming to a wedding, christening or funeral at the Church Support Hub, for school groups at Scripture Union, and for tourists at Church Care and Churches Visitor & Tourism Association.[21]

- If you have a Wi-Fi code, clearly display it so that people don't feel bad checking their phones or taking photos. Some churches use QR codes for a tourist trail,[22] or an app.[23]
- Take a cue from pubs and cafes and put a dog bowl outside if you welcome pets.
- Basic but important: if you have the opportunity to talk, gently ask people what brought them to your church and if there's anything particular they're looking for. Don't just talk about why you come and all the things you like about your church. It's about them, not just about you!

Historical heritage

- Free booklets explaining architectural features are available from CPO and others. If you're creating it yourself, aim for accessible language.
- Coventry Cathedral has worked with York's Centre for the Study of Christianity and Culture to create an interactive app guide. Others have used local app developers, even for virtual reality versions of historic buildings.
- The following words are in a tourist leaflet for a historical church, which has a map and photo trail along with a photo of the congregation and a letter:

I am reminded almost daily of the weight of history in this church and throughout the village. The church building displays in so many ways the inspirational story of a community, willingly sacrificing themselves for the sake of others. It also bears witness to another act of great sacrifice, the Christian message that God so loved the world that he gave his Son Jesus Christ to die upon the cross. It is this message that continues to motivate the church family that meets to this day. To find out more see our website.[24]

Connection made: past, present, everlasting.

Social justice

- Follow many other churches in becoming an eco-church, with full support from the charity A Rocha, or celebrate 'Creationtide' in the autumn. Small steps might be as simple as using LED light bulbs. Telling people you are doing this speaks volumes about Christians' care for the planet.
- Set up a fair trade stall, or offer Fairtrade coffee.[25]
- Have a foodbank collection point within the church, particularly at harvest. CPO produce foodbank publicity.

- Have a place in the building with information for those in crisis or poverty, perhaps from local charities with which you have a relationship.

One church, when a homeless man became a regular member of the congregation, was inspired to start running suppers for the homeless: 'a venture into the unknown but we've had an amazing response'.[26] In Brighton 14 churches join together to offer a night-shelter scheme over four months. When they heard about it at a carol service more visitors volunteered to help than there were spaces. It communicated love in action. It communicated that the church cares. It communicated that God cares.

The centrality of the gospel

- Everyone who visits should have a way of finding out more afterwards, whether that's a website address or a contact card.
- Have a library of good spiritual books for people to read and return; some even have little laminated book reviews or recommendations. For inspiration on the power of reading a good Christian book, check out www.booksforlife.uk.
- Scripture presented as art or graphic design will capture people's attention. CPO offer a range of

styles, as do the artists on preditos.com and many others. Framing the designs communicates value and looks better. They work well in a hall or even behind the toilet door. Posters with provoking questions may prompt a conversation.

- There has been a resurgence in what some call 'tracts', 'outreach booklets', or 'gospel giveaways'. Have new stock available. They're not expensive, and they could change someone's life.[27] Lifewords (previously Scripture Gift Mission) and Gospel Imprints also provide free material.

- Look for ways in displays to describe the qualities of God and faith that people seek as they come. Do you want to say 'We are great', or 'God is great'?

In summary

What is your core message? Imagine you're new. Walk into church, look around, sit through a service, then finish this sentence: 'I can tell this is a church that…'

3. Who is our focus?

Everyone! Of course. Narrowing it down, however, can actually make you better ultimately at reaching everyone. As well as the learning styles explored on page 11 there are four other areas to consider: neighbourhood, culture, generation and language.

Neighbourhood. The book on websites in this series talked about the 'personas' that marketing organisations use to identify a typical person they are trying to reach. To keep hearing the voice of those not in the church you could use the tools listed at the back to find data about your neighbours and build a picture of your community, or explore some of the ideas in *Church from the Outside* in this series.

Visitors look for a point of connection, a 'touch point'. Demonstrate a working understanding of what's going on in the local area, reference local news or characters, favourite places or communal gatherings, because it communicates that the church is integral to community life, not a holy huddle. Think about one of your church neighbours. If this person came, what would be their route to genuine engagement and connection?

Culture. As you consider your neighbourhood, you'll find yourself identifying its cultural quirks. Two questions to ask:

- How does what we offer fit into people's lives?
- What 'comfort zones' could we create?

The culture of our church can connect or disconnect in subtle ways. Look at the success of Fresh Expressions churches, which have grown in the face of decline in other areas. Often focused on a homogenous group, they demonstrate a high awareness of cultural needs and norms. A study of over 500 fresh expressions found that nearly half of their people had not previously attended church. Encouragingly, there are four times as many fresh expressions of church starting now compared with ten years ago.[28]

The visual designs we use can put people off any expression of church. CPO has worked hard to increase the breadth of the designs it offers to churches, because a stock photo and cheesy pun might make one person smile, but most will cringe. If the visual quality and designs in your church are extremely different from anything you'd see anywhere else in your area this is not necessarily a good thing!

I liked this story from the book *Church Marketing 101*:

A woman is driving down a pitch-dark road late at night and sees she is almost out of gas. Her fear is somewhat relieved as she sees two gas stations up ahead. If these two stations are equally accessible, and the gas is equally priced, which will she choose? Simple. She will choose the one with better lighting. Why? At that moment her primary need is safety. Better lighting makes her feel safer. Her response is natural—just as natural as the first conclusions that people commonly draw about churches. Imagine the owner of the less-frequented one. He tries to solve the problem by dropping prices, hiring a new graphic designer, making a new sign and increasing stock, but his sales do not increase. He is missing the connection. He doesn't understand what drives people.[29]

We need to understand what drives the people we're trying to reach.

Generation. The older you are, the more likely you are to believe Jesus actually walked the earth, but the less likely you are to talk about him. The younger you are, the more likely you are to talk about Jesus, but the less likely you are to read your Bible, pray or attend church.[30] Research into 'millennials' found that although a third found church 'boring', two-thirds of them described church as 'a place to find answers to live a meaningful life'. However, welcome teams take note, they are freaked out when you ask for their name, address, email address and mobile number on a first visit.[31]

There isn't the space here to address how to communicate to different generations—you will have your own practices, which may become more effective if you can assess them—but as one writer points out, for the first time we now find five generations in church together: 'Go young or grow old together—both benefit the Kingdom of God. Just don't fool yourself into thinking you can do both.'[32]

However, the risk of communication bias to one group is that some feel more valued than others. Martyn Payne has pointed out with reference to Messy Church that churches are called to be inherently intergenerational places, where all ages relate as fellow children of God.[33] Recent research has confirmed that 'young adults'—anyone over the age of 16, but I'd go younger than that—want to be treated as equal members of the church, not artificially separated out.[34] A word of warning against using 'cool' language for teens or weird text abbreviations. As Nicola David puts it in her Grove book on publicity and the local church, 'Teenagers can spot cheesiness from miles away, and churches can be good at cheese-making.'[35] Oh yes.

Where possible, ask for people's communication preferences. Perhaps people prefer text to email.

Apart from it just being polite to ask, it's now acknowledged in marketing and fundraising that people are more likely to respond if they are in control of how they're contacted. Chapter 4 has church database suggestions and advice on data protection. A careful database is crucial.

Language. Watch out for jargon and too many words. If the magazine articles are all dense with prose they may not get read, so actually you won't be communicating anything at all. Silly language risks communicating that a church knows it is irrelevant. The overly pious risks communicating that a church is there to chastise.

If people speak English as an additional language, consider information in multiple languages. Simple language will reach more people.

I've seen the following in a couple of places, with some regional differences. This is language which, in the right context, really tries to connect:

Welcome to those who are single, married, divorced, widowed, gay, confused, filthy rich, comfortable or dirt poor. Welcome if you are from the north, south, or just passing by. Welcome if you can sing like Pavarotti or can't sing a note. Welcome if you're 'just browsing', just woke up, or just got out of prison. Welcome if you're more Christian than the Archbishop of Canterbury, or haven't been in church since little Jack's christening. Welcome if you are still in recovery or still addicted. Welcome if you're having problems or you're down in the dumps or if you don't like 'organised religion', if you blew all your money on the horses, if you work too hard, don't work, don't know anything about 'church' or are only here because grandma is in town and she wanted to go to church. Welcome if you could use a prayer right now, if you had religion shoved down your throat as a child or if you've lived here all your life just never been in. Welcome seekers and doubters, saints and sinners, regulars, visitors, friends and strangers.[36]

4. Are we communicating a cohesive, consistent, credible identity?

Advice from one church consultant: 'Don't chase cool. Don't out-trend yourself. Once it's created and implemented, be consistent. Consistency tells people you are trustworthy and not flaky. I was part of a church that had three different logos in two years. Were we going through an identity crisis? Yep.'[37]

One of the purposes of the 'pile of printed materials' exercise earlier was to look for shared values, so that different communication tools, ministries and activities are not trying to out-shout each other, but instead are part of a cohesive whole.

A regular tricky request to CPO is a design showing lots of faces of normal-looking people, smiling, different ages, colours and classes, British. In other words, a perfect stock photo of who we want to be.

The problem is that if it's not who we actually are, then it risks irrelevance at best, hypocrisy at worst. What do people want a church to communicate? Authenticity. What do we want to communicate? Christ—and the good news is that he is always authentic. If we're true to him, and as true as we can be to who we are, then we stand a greater chance of communicating a cohesive, consistent and therefore credible identity.

5. Are our expectations realistic and shared?

It's not enough to paint a vision of how wonderful it could be. Motivation to change also requires dissatisfaction with the present. You'll need at least one meeting which brings together decision-makers in church leadership with those involved in all aspects of church communication: external, internal, print, digital.

Use the questions in this book to identify priorities, then be honest together about your expectations on aims, costs and timescales. If this group can share a vision for what needs to be achieved it will be far easier to convince any doubters in the congregation.

Everyone will benefit from a regular conversation to plan and ensure everything matches as much as possible. One person passionate about banning typos and grammatical errors might be willing to do this for every communication type. Another person with a real eye for graphic design can ensure standards are high across the board.

Expectations grow once communication starts to change. It may be that you start with a few token gestures on the walls, or redesign the weekly newssheet or update. If this causes revolution, then there are bigger issues to address. If the only comments are mildly positive then the path is clear.

3

Essential next steps

So far we've tried to hone the vision, and shape a strategy. Now for the plan. You'll see a list of 15 tools. Some will be ripe for use now; others need to wait for another season… (I'm feeling an agricultural metaphor coming on… some could be farmed out?) Some will take more time, or more courage, to deploy because they are part of the 'structure' we described in chapter 1. That's the music metaphor: where the rhythm can be varied a bit, the creative flourishes are your chance to show off. You'll know which of these communication tools has most potential for sowing the seeds and singing the song. (Yes, I really do like a metaphor.)

Have you come across this?

Sow a thought, and you reap an act;
Sow an act, and you reap a habit;
Sow a habit, and you reap a character;
Sow a character, and you reap a destiny.[38]

This chapter suggests these steps:

- Choose your tool—15 are described in detail
- Choose your look
- Plan your year
- Plan your content
- Find your team

Choose your tool

These pages go through some of the communication tools at your disposal inside the church.

First, the ones that are likely to be most ingrained: buildings, including use of art and light, seating and an additional note on cathedrals, community spaces, internal noticeboards, banners and wall hangings, signage and wayfinding, coffee, books and tables, music, preaching.

Next, the rhythms: news-sheet, magazine, prayer diary. Finally, some excuses for creative flourish: welcome packs, stories and testimonies, videos.

For ideas around common core values to communicate (prayer, world mission, children and young people, welcoming locals, welcoming one-time visitors, historical heritage, social justice, the centrality of the gospel), see pages 23–32.

1. A new look at the architecture

Buildings are not as immovable as we think. Any church that has invested in a more 'open' entrance will tell you the difference it can make.

Most churches were built with theological and cultural intention. Setting aside a time to recall and reflect on this can unlock creative use of the space. If you need to make structural changes to your building, there are others who have learned valuable lessons about almost any change you'd want to make, from mezzanine floors to internal glass walls, replacing pews with chairs or dark backdrops with light. Chapter 4 points to resources to help you.

One church in Grantham has really pulled out the stops at Advent. It has tried an ice rink inside the church, a real ale festival, and has a temporary ski slope planned. Father Stuart Cradduck told the press, 'Of course it will always be a sacred space, but as well as that, we hope that everyone will rediscover it as a community resource for everyone;' and to the BBC he added, 'Let's do something unexpected. Be something different and challenge people's conceptions about who we are and what we are doing.'[39] Yes—the church has grown as a result, and perceptions have undoubtedly changed.

Art and light

Cathedrals have set a standard in the use of contemporary art to challenge, inspire and prompt worship. Find networks that support this in chapter 4. Lighting can transform a traditional building. Candles can be used traditionally in worship, particularly in celebrations of Candlemas, but there are plenty of alternative uses too.[40] One Baptist church used ropes across the balcony to lower a candle in a lantern past the pulpit to the floor, representing the Light of the World come down to us. A young man looking for work experience in his chosen career of theatre lighting was given an opportunity in one church over Christmas, with magical results. More simply, ground-level internal spotlights, fairy lights, freestanding spotlights and LED battery-powered lights which come on when they sense movement can be cheap, portable and hugely effective, literally lighting the way to church.

Seating

Like many others before her, a friend decided to rediscover her Catholic roots when her children were small. She's an interior designer. What did she first notice? 'The fixed seating. It's solid. Familiar. Grounded. I'm so glad they're not movable. If they were, what would be there next time I come?' For the churches who long to 'get rid of the pews', this is worth remembering! Seating in straight lines can communicate performance; seating 'in the round' communicates participation. If you have pews, could they be comfier? If you have kneelers or cushions, are they embroidered meaningfully or beautifully? If you have moveable seats make the most of the flexibility.

Non-traditional church buildings

It's not just fresh expressions and church plants that use schools, warehouses and hotels as church buildings. There are churches meeting in cinemas and theatres where the congregation has outgrown buildings. If this is your situation you may be more conscious of the challenges than the opportunities ('nowhere to store stuff!' say the hardest-working audiovisual teams in Christendom). Use digital displays, which are easier now with tools like Adobe Spark and small projectors. Industrial buildings can be transformed by some large-format vinyl. Portable roll-up banners can be interchangeable and affordable—and consider mini ones and illuminated ones too.[41] You are free from ancient noticeboards and woodworm. There are benefits.

Cathedrals

Cathedrals also often make frequent use of portable roll-up banners, but in other respects they are different from ordinary churches. As Simon Jenkins writes in his 2016 book on cathedrals, 'Millions who have no commitment to Christianity are drawn to their embrace, to feel their spirits uplifted by beauty.' He notes that a quarter of non-religious British adults have made a visit in the past year.

Amid an emphasis in church growth programmes on personal welcome and assimilation, Jenkins makes an interesting point about 'the attraction of what sociologist Grace Davie ascribed to cathedrals as "vicarious religion… the desire for anonymity, the option to come and go without explanation or commitment".'[42] Michael Palin has written of stumbling across a church in the midst of a hectic day: 'I was never so grateful for a place of repose, an oasis of peace and quiet in the midst of the mayhem.'[43] We mustn't forget that some choose not to visit smaller local churches for fear of getting ambushed into volunteering. Cathedrals and ancient buildings serve us all as places of retreat as well as places of worship.

2. Community use

Among British adults 83% recognise the importance of churches as community spaces.[44] We can then assume that most of our neighbours, irrespective of their beliefs, have a vested interest in keeping church buildings in good nick: warm, not smelly, child-friendly, with toilets, a functioning kitchen, lighting, disabled access, in 'good decorative order', no peeling paint, no lead stolen from the roof, and no stones crumbling on to the street. For churches that need to fundraise and are building a case for support, the message to neighbours is not a plea to 'help us', but to 'support your local community by helping your local church'.

The National Churches Trust offer great support on this, and help with funding proposals too. There are more suggestions in chapter 4. Strikingly, their survey showed that the more the building is cared for, the more people volunteer, not to keep the church nice, but for the mission of the church and its community activities. It's a virtuous circle: invest in the building, more people use it, and the community builds a network of support and friendship. This in turn encourages investment in the building.[45] Some churches even raise funds by using the building as a bed and breakfast—church camping, or 'champing'.[46]

It's not always simple, but others have been there before and can offer advice and templates for you to use, including, for example, checklists and documents for using halls for the community (see chapter 4).[47] If your building is listed, and even if it's not, changes may require a Permission/Faculty under the Ecclesiastical Exemption. You'll need to complete a Statement of Significance and a Statement of Need. Church of England, Catholic, Methodist, Baptist and URC churches are exempted from some parts of planning legislation, but not all—and permission needs to be obtained from their denomination rather than the government planning authorities. Allow more time than you'd first assume.[48] The Historic Religious Buildings Alliance has produced a list of resources to provide help and advice for those looking after historic religious buildings, or running a project to adapt them for community use. They say on their website, 'We think this is really useful!' They're right—it really is. Some of the content is summarised in chapter 4, or use the link www.hrballiance.org.uk/resources/help-advice for the full list.

3. Internal noticeboards

Remove any meeting minutes, rotas, insurance certificates or internal newsletters from the board most likely to be seen by visitors. Distribute them another way, or put them somewhere discreet for collection. If the backing of the board looks ugly and you can't either afford a new one or remove it entirely, cover the whole space with one backing poster. Find someone who loves straightening everything up, arranging the contents in neat groups and making sure it communicates that this is a church that pays attention to detail!

You may want a local community board for local events, jobs, requests, etc. If this is entirely separate from the church board, it's a great place to incorporate information about church events. Also exercise regular 'editorial control' (otherwise known as the executive privilege of 'filing things in the bin'). What is there really does reflect on the church.

Portable boards can create display areas out of dead wall space. Some display ideas from other churches:

- photos of people involved in church life, including names if you have their permission (you may need to recruit a designated photographer)

- photos of activities during the week with big speech bubble quotes from participants
- maps of places the church prays for, including a local map, perhaps with written prayers
- posters from organisations the church supports. Even better, say next to it how the church offers support, or how people can get involved.
- interactive child-friendly displays, which can help communicate that all ages are integral to the life of the church (see page 26).

4. Posters, wall art and banners

Art on a wall says more than brick. Words on a wall say more than paint. So why are we so conservative in our decoration of churches? Here are some options for breaking away from the brown and beige:

Handmade textile banners

These can, as professional church textile artist Juliet Hemingray says, 'take a seed of an idea and make something that is not only a visual aid to worship but also something of quality and beauty that will speak of the fullness and richness of the Gospel of Christ'.[49] At their best, textiles can be simply stunning. Aim for the best, so that you don't mind when it's still there in five years' time.

Handmade posters and banners

If these are either collaged by hand or produced quickly on the church computer, they sometimes escape sound objective judgement on their quality because we don't want to hurt people's feelings, or diminish the time they've freely decided to spend. Understandable, but not excusable in something as important as what we communicate as a church. There are digital tools to help.[50] Sometimes an obviously amateur effort doesn't matter, but it may actually cost less in time, and less than you'd expect in budget, to do it professionally. Here's how:

Professional design

Do you want a design that is good to go (no changes necessary) or 'customisable' (flexible space for your details)? If you're adding your details, aim for simplicity, legibility and only the most relevant details, perhaps pointing people to a website for more. The reason the vast majority of CPO's banners and posters are customisable is because we all have something specific we want to say to our particular community. They all have guidelines on the best spacing, fonts and colours so that the finished version is likely to come out looking professional, even if you're not a professional designer.

Chapter 4 includes some questions to answer before you brief a graphic designer. The 'tighter' the brief, the fewer amends, and the lower the cost, in both time and money. Contrary to popular expectation, designers are not mind-readers, but they may come up with something better than what you had in mind.

Next, decide on size and material. Paper, tear-proof paper, laminated or vinyl? Many will pay more for something weather and fade-proof. Roll-up banners are portable and come in different sizes and qualities, and sometimes you can keep the stand but replace the graphic. Illuminated banners are great in dark spaces. Banners can hang from eyelets or clips using bungees. I am a fan of 'snap frames', where the four sides snap open so the contents can be changed without using screws or wall fittings. Arrangements of white frames can look as good in a church foyer as they would in your hall at home.

Finally, look at printing options. Some churches have invested in high-quality colour printers. These can work well for posters if the quality is high, and you've factored in the cost of ink and time as well as that of the machine itself. Printing in-house like this can cost more than you realise, but can also be efficient for posters; it is probably not possible for banners.

Four questions to ask on print:

1. Is there the option to pay for the design and print in one go? You can for CPO designs and for some others. In many cases it can save time.
2. Do I have time to find the lowest price? You will find some very low print prices online, but may need to sacrifice quality and delivery times. Some also require a minimum quantity. As designers say, everyone wants it good, fast and cheap, but you'll only ever get two out of the three.
3. What do I need to do to prepare the file for print? Most printers prefer a high-resolution PDF file with crop marks and 3 mm bleed (the design extends 3 mm over what will be the edge, so that when it's cut there aren't any white marks). If you have particular ('bespoke') requirements such as special paper or unusual sizes or quantities, you'll need to be clear on these before you get a quote. A good printer will tell you if your images are not at print quality. As a most basic guideline, images less than 1 MB aren't going to cut it in any poster or banner. For something as large as a banner they need to be 300 dpi. These are all areas in which a professional service is helpful.
4. Are relationship and shared values important to you? Those who know the owners of a local,

independent print shop will be aware of this. At CPO I'm always grateful for those who've realised that printing with a Christian charity gives us the ability to continue serving more churches.

Even the best printer in the world can't compensate for a pixelated image or for bad design. Sorry.

5. Signage and wayfinding

This is so often neglected, but notice in public buildings the commercial investment in signs, 'wayfinding' as it's called, because it puts 'customer usability' first. Think about sightlines. When you walk, where do you look? Probably above people's heads for direction, and at waist level for information. If it's your first time, where do your eyes go to find the exits, hall, toilet, coffee, information?

You can buy permanent signs to mount above doorways on all walls. Here are some other ideas:

- A-boards and pull-up banners are great for entrances if they won't hinder access.
- Typography painted or stencilled on to a wall.
- Digital signage (a screen with directions and information) can be as simple as a TV screen connected to a PowerPoint via Wi-Fi. People who can advise on this are listed in chapter 4.

- A handmade stand with direction posts can work well, or hanging chalk boards mounted on hooks.
- Some churches use large polystyrene, block or card letters to spell out 'WELCOME', 'LOVE' or 'HOLY'. These are creative, portable and can be really striking when combined with candles.

6. Coffee, books and tables

Make sure there's space for take-away information, on a table or bookshelf. Perspex stands are a good investment, particularly if they are kept tidy. Be ruthless about making sure that what is there reflects those you're trying to reach, and be clear about what is on sale, what is free and what invites a donation.

Increasingly churches are offering tea and coffee during the week, not just after the service. Church coffee shops and cafes, often with a bookshop attached, are a blessing to the community, to Christian book publishing and to evangelism.

One volunteer from a church cafe in London, 'Host', says, 'We are open to people from all walks of life, and unlike other coffee houses, we do not insist on people buying coffee to stay here, so we are opening up the church as a public "third space"'. It is clearly working. Andrew, who works nearby, says,

'I've always hated coffee shops, so I come here for the atmosphere. I am new to the church and have started coming to services.'[51] Resources to explore this are in chapter 4.

7. Music

Music in church—whether you love yours or despair of it—can act as the word of God sung in people's heads all week long. Communal singing is both medically and spiritually therapeutic, even when the tune or words are not what you'd prefer. Tunes are memorable; sermons often aren't. With a phone and a small speaker, recorded music or backing tracks give more flexibility than ever before to churches without musicians or churches wanting some ambient tunes rather than a hymn. Music is powerful even when it's not perfect. Conferences and digital resources can help inspire your worship team.[52]

(A note on nurturing musicians in churches: start young. I have yet to meet a 13-year-old boy who wouldn't rather be behind a bass guitar or drum kit than in the pew. Even if they're not the most musical, even if the sound is turned off, it's worth it. I've known young people come to faith from 'helping out' in the most welcoming and gracious weekly gig in town—at their local church.)

8. Preaching

The sermon, message, homily… for anyone visiting your church, the communication in the central talk may well be the lasting impression, whether it's five or 50 minutes long. Obviously this is not just the content, whether expository, thematic or very blatantly off the top of someone's head. The tone, the warmth, the body language, the level of conviction will all communicate just as much, if not more.

Creative preachers will be aware of the types of learning mentioned on page 11. They'll use props, move around, perhaps invite participation or application of some kind. They'll think carefully about the shape of their words, and may encourage people to take notes or doodle, even on their phone. A relevant talk communicates more powerfully than any amount of decoration around it. One study across UK denominations found that 96.9% of respondents look forward to the sermon, and three-quarters found sermons helped them understand current events.[53]

Some advice intended for corporate presentations can be appropriated here, like these questions that acknowledge the needs of those listening:

- Trust the driver; why should they listen to me? Who am I, beyond labels?
- What is expected of them; what are they going to have to do?
- What are they going to get as a result of listening?
- Are they being seen and acknowledged?[54]

A survey by Christian Research in 2016 found that nine out of ten churchgoers enjoy sermons, but want fewer (presumably bad) jokes from preachers.[55] There are some excellent books on preaching, and *Preach* magazine focuses on this neglected but crucial area of church communication, providing a breadth of contributors on preaching themes and also book reviews.[56] If you put sermons on your website, assume that Christians considering coming to your church will have a listen before they come.

9. Weekly news-sheet

Whether or not they email news or put it online, most churches have some form of handout, with a short welcome, a summary of what is happening on a Sunday, key 'notices', information and possibly some space for sermon notes. Some churches also include a prayer for the local area or the world, a who's who with pictures, or a tear-off contact form.

A5, or A4 folded, is probably big enough. Colour is a bonus but not essential. Pictures and images are great, but don't stretch them, or use them if they're fuzzy or pixelated, or use copyright pictures without permission, including random images from the internet. Often 'cutout' pictures against a white background, or 'vectors', are better than something fixed within a grey box. PowerPoint actually has a very simple tool to remove the background on an image, which you may find handy before you copy and paste it into your news-sheet.

Some churches use term cards instead, with key dates. If you're going to the trouble of printing the information and it is intended to have a shelf life of more than a week, then make the most of the effort by also including some vision in there too—the 'why' as well as the 'what', or perhaps some prayers.

Seven tips to keep print information fresh and simple:

- For information notices, cut the waffle and prioritise in this order: what, when, where. For example: pancake party, Tues 9 Feb, 7.00–9.00 pm, Pastor Dave's house. Contact office@ churchwebsite.org.uk or call XXXXXX for address/ directions. Always include the day as well as the date, since our weekly calendars rule everything.

- Don't feel you need to include everything submitted. If it's only relevant to a small number they could be told in person or another way. If you ever think, 'How small can I make the type and still get away with it?' you have too much information.
- Consider including screenshots of your church website or social media if you have them, and clear ways for people to find them.
- Keep the logo and church name at the top consistent with all your other communication. No more than two fonts—one for headings, one for 'body text'.
- Line everything up. It may seem fiddly, but it will look better. No more than two columns, and plenty of white space.
- Some churches offer paper handouts only to visitors, and use weekly emails for regulars—but use the website as repository for most of the information.
- If you're putting your news-sheet on the website or emailing it out, make sure it's saved and uploaded as a PDF file so that everyone can open it. There is more on this in the 'Church Online' books in this series.

10. Magazines

In 2016 I surveyed 70 UK church magazine editors and discovered that most magazines are A5 (83%), put together with Word or Publisher (78%), printed at home or church, come out ten to twelve times a year, and cost a notional amount. Although some print thousands of copies, most churches produce around 150, which are available in the church and elsewhere. The companion book in this series (*Church from the Outside*) explores the community reach of our magazines. If large companies such as Argos continue to invest in print even with a fully functioning website, then we can safely assume that print magazines are here to stay alongside digital communication. By 'hanging around' in kitchen piles they play their part—an important one—as a tangible expression of church community.

It is encouraging that as well as the obligatory 'letter from the vicar', the vast majority of magazines include photos and local news, and a third include interviews with local people and a children's section. This communicates that the church is part of the local community, not set apart.

Churches need to remember the reach of the magazine to the 'audience at the back', the friends and family who idly pick it up and browse. The toolkit has resources to assist church editors with the practicalities, and much of the advice about print and design on pages 51–54 also applies to magazines.

Take time once in a while to look at the subtext rather than the text. In other words, forget the grammar for a moment and ask what is communicated overall. Is the subtext actually negative? Are you accidentally communicating that you are a clique of people who all look the same, that religion is full of rituals, that people outside the church are judged, patronised or a target for conversion? Does it look like Christians think they have all the answers, when those reading probably have doubts?

Conversely, a magazine is a chance to communicate that the church is active in helping the poor, that Christians are aware of needs around the world. It can show that prayer seems to have an impact on people's lives, and people in church are welcoming of everyone. Stories can communicate that God is relevant to people today in the place where I live, the Bible says some interesting stuff, people in church have a sense of humour, and they clearly care. This is a story worth telling, and a message worth the effort of compiling, designing and printing a magazine.

For layout, the advice is similar to the news-sheet above, and in the 'Choose your look' section on page 70: align things neatly; don't use too many fonts or illustration styles; embrace 'white space' around headings and images so that people can read it as easily as possible; and keep the look and feel consistent throughout. That's not boring; it's more stylish, and more likely to get read.

11. Prayer diaries

Prayer diaries are a great example of how email and print can work together. A regular email and handout with prayer requests can strengthen community. It's always a good moment when you finally meet someone you've been praying for. Prayer diaries are great for information, but their main benefit is prayer! We need it! Intersperse the personal (the congregation and any activities they're involved in), the local (events, activities, streets, authorities) and the national (issues, government, charities, events) with the global (but get permission for anything you say about missionaries for security reasons). Use full names wherever appropriate and pictures if possible. Keep it short and sweet. Use Bible verses too. Be aware that it could be picked up by anyone, so if in doubt, keep it out.

12. PowerPoint

Churches with screens, projectors and internet access have more communication options. Some screens roll in for a service; some roll down from the ceiling and are invisible for most of the week. Some churches just use a TV on wheels. If these seem like they'd be inappropriate or inaccessible in your building, or you have technical questions about projector options, there are organisations listed in chapter 4 who can advise, or you can use video and presentations on people's phones instead, by putting them on a website and sharing via email or social media.

If you have a screen, have you tried using PowerPoint (or perhaps the alternative: Keynote, on a Mac, or Prezi, with all its exciting moving features and a month's free trial) in all of the areas below? Here are some ideas from other churches:

Welcome: You could use clear website links, pictures from during the week, notices in other languages, a summary of what will happen in the service, information for children, an invitation to tea and coffee, or perhaps a prayer of preparation for the service.

Sermon points: No more than twelve words on the screen at any one time is the standard guideline. Clear points to 'navigate' the talk (not necessarily all beginning with the same letter) can be more memorable on screen when they are imperative ('Pray without ceasing') or a personalised question ('When do I pray?') rather than just headings ('Continual prayer'). A strong image can speak volumes[57] but don't leave it up for too long or it'll become distracting. Don't spend too long preparing the PowerPoint—it's not the main point, and you're not trying to impress anyone. Therefore, no moving animations, no Word Art, no rotating text, and please (please!) no 'fun' slide transitions. If sermon slides draw attention to themselves it's at the risk of distracting rather than serving the message.

Notices: Commercial advice on presentation skills is helpful here. There are three elements: you, your material, and your 'audience', who, let's face it, may well be thinking about something else. A screen helps with focus and visual reinforcement, but a connection with the 'audience' requires you to think about their needs and establish a connection: mention someone's name, or empathise, or motivate them to listen, perhaps putting a photo on screen in anticipation.

Liturgy and scripture: There's something about all speaking the same words in the same direction, rather than all looking down into a book, which speaks of our unity in Christ.[58] Screens provide a way of doing this, and help include those for whom the words or physical Bibles are unfamiliar.

Prayer: Consider images from the news while praying for the country and the world, or photos of people and groups. Written prayers spoken together or read in silence can be really effective, with or without images (and better no image than a bad or cheesy one).

Song lyrics: It's far easier to use specialist software for this, and if you're starting out the resources in chapter 4 may help.[59] It can be nerve-racking for operators. I was responsible for the song words on the laptop once; my mind drifted, and suddenly I realised no one was singing and the guy at the front was raising both eyebrows at me. Oops. So, some top tips from the experienced: as soon as people start singing the final word on the screen, move on. Whoever is leading may well have a different order in mind, or a printout with different words, so check beforehand. Memorise the shortcut to the chorus. Sing along. If it isn't working, check the connections, uncheck and check the 'display' option, and if desperate, as anyone who's seen the *IT Crowd* on TV will know, just turn it off and on again. If all else fails, sing something well known or repetitive, copy and paste from the internet into PowerPoint, or type fast!

13. Welcome place

I've visited churches in Kenya where newcomers are invited to stand up and say where they've come from. I've visited churches in the US where the welcome desk is akin to a five-star-hotel reception desk. However yours looks, it is helpful to have a designated place for people to come of their own accord. It gives newcomers something to do if no one is saying hello. It needs to be clearly visible ('Connection Point', 'Welcome Table').

Here are some of the things I've seen that show evidence of thought and care:

- A simple card on chairs that can be exchanged at the desk for a full welcome pack, with matching design but more detail
- Paper bags, stickered or printed, with leaflets and maybe sweets or chocolate
- A pile of postcards tied together with yarn with introductions and details of what goes on, some more time-specific than others

The welcome postcard template used by CPO tries to take the best of those we've seen: name, date, address, postcode, phone number, little boxes like this ☐☐☐☐☐ for the email address (because otherwise it'll probably be illegible), preferred form of communication, and the question 'How can we help you?' (prayer requests, questions, comments). It needs to say what you will do with the information, for example: 'We'd like to stay in touch. Are you happy for us to keep your contact details securely stored on our database?' There are resources on data protection and church databases listed in chapter 4. Make sure your email lists are kept separate, so that someone only interested in carol services doesn't suddenly start receiving emails with prayer requests.

14. Stories and testimonies

Christians in church have amazing stories to tell of God's faithfulness, guidance and power. In adult baptism services these are routinely shared. In regular services they are sometimes absent altogether. After a missions trip there may be big stories to tell, but the seemingly insignificant anecdote about normal, day-to-day life as a Christian may have immense power in someone else's life. If you need inspiration, look at the stories on the Evangelical Alliance's 'Great

Commission' website, or at www.yesheis.com, from Christian Vision. Stories in person are wonderful, because they invite discussion and follow-up, but stories on video from the internet are available too. Which leads neatly into:

15. Video

There are three formats for showing video: streamed video (a link from YouTube), professional video downloads (from Vimeo or a church 'stock' site such as Worship House Media[60]) or something home-grown, perhaps filmed on a phone, perhaps edited on the kind of software that is now taught in primary school. Streaming will require a decent internet connection, and downloads are always worth checking before the service. Editing home/phone video using free tools such as iMovie and cheap apps like Videohance can produce good results.

General advice on using video in services is the same as for 'shareable content' on social media: for length, ideally 30 seconds, and rarely more than two minutes. Movie clips can work well but you may need to check about copyright. 'Talking heads' are made far more interesting with the simple addition of a clip-on microphone and movement, and perhaps a photo interspersed, or narration over a video slideshow. There are plenty of online tutorials to teach you how to add text, graphics and music, and apps that will do most of the work for you. There's more advice about this in the digital communications books in this series.

There we go: 15 tools, and there may be others you can use too. After you've chosen your tool, you can choose your look, plan your year, plan your content and find your team.

Choose your look

A solid aim for printed communication inside church is that even if it doesn't match, it looks as though it has come from the same family. It saves time too.

This is achievable, for instance, by:

- Always put the church name or logo in the top left.
- Always put contacts or website at the bottom.
- Using the same font for 'body text' in everything, printed and on a screen. Standard choices include Arial, Gill Sans, Verdana, Calibri, Franklin Gothic and Open Sans. Aim for no more than three fonts on anything printed. Comic Sans is fine for

children, but is disliked by every graphic designer I've met. All the fonts in CPO's online overprint tool work on any computer system and have been chosen by a group of church designers because they can make posters and banners look good.

- For headline fonts, or fonts on PowerPoint, choose something appropriate for your church. You could go minimalist, or try the handwriting 'vintage' that is so popular (at the time of writing!). If you're trying to attract young people you might steer clear of the more traditional stock photography.

There is a free download with examples from Nicola David to accompany her Grove booklet on Publicity and the Local Church available at bit.ly/ GrovePublicity.

If you don't have a logo, or want to update your logo, you'll probably need a budget, a designer, and as clear as possible an idea of any colours, images or words you definitely do or don't want. There are organisations who specialise in this listed in chapter 4. A good church logo is simple (not too many colours), works at different sizes, is flexible enough to work against different colour backgrounds, and has an appropriate font for the style of the community.

You might need to standardise the words you use to refer to the church, the church network, your mission statement or your values. My church uses the acronym FREE: Following Jesus, Reaching Out, Extended Family, doing Everything in Love.

There are rules about photos that I'd hope would be obvious: don't stretch them out of proportion; do make sure they're high enough resolution; don't take them off the internet unless you are certain you have permission from the photographer; do credit any photographers in the church; don't use photos of kids; do use photos that tell a story, not just cheesy grins or atmospheric waterfalls.

Every brand you recognise will probably have a 'style guide' with detailed rules on use of the logo, type and language. This wouldn't be necessary for most churches, but the thinking behind them is helpful. Ideally you will look at any communication and know very quickly that it's yours.

Plan your year

If you're bringing in new ideas you might need to cut back on other things to create slack in the system, and release capacity. Could your weekly news-sheet be replaced by a term card or magazine page, with updates online, on text, or said on a Sunday? Could your welcome information for newcomers be made less time-sensitive, so that it needs replacing less frequently? Could it point to the website or somewhere else for the latest contact details or dates? There's a limit to this. It still needs to be relevant. Could your magazine jump down the frequency scale to be termly, quarterly or bi-monthly?

It's safe to allow six weeks for communication to filter to everyone, dates to get in the diaries, and invites to be given out. Plan communications by counting back further than you'd think. Think 'cross-stream' and 'multiplatform', as the corporate world would put it. You're effectively running a mini campaign, so cover all the bases: posters, banners, invites, flyers, decorating the building, website, social media, plugs from the front, email, text, stories and of course creative flourishes, which may take up most energy, but could have the most impact.

At my church we have created an internal rhythm of two gift days—for world mission in May, and local mission in November. These are 'big Sundays'. There are no traditional fundraising activities, but there's a large amount of storytelling, often a little prayer booklet produced in the church office for the week leading up to the gift day, sometimes videos, sometimes little Facebook stories, sometimes a teaching series, and a good four weeks' notice, because not everyone comes every week.

Your special services might include baptisms, christenings, confirmations, first communions, weddings and funerals. Every week 6,000 families visit Church of England churches for christenings, weddings or funerals. The Church Support Hub is intended to help them, but can be used by any denomination to help churches make the most of these services, with printed resources at www.churchprinthub.org. It helps when regular church members make the effort to attend life events too to welcome guests, who may even come again.

Are there new rhythms you'd like to introduce in your communications and church calendar? Could you reshape your regular rhythms to give 'air' in your communications for the messages that matter most?

Plan your content

When creating designs at CPO we're very aware of the difference between those that are intended to provoke people and those that are intended to bless them. Sometimes they're about welcome. Sometimes they're an invitation. The tone may be very different. Here are some values that churches have used to help them plan the tone of their content:

- Talk about 'you' not 'us'. So, instead of saying, 'Join us,' say 'This is your church.' Instead of 'We need this,' say, 'You might find this interesting.'
- Make it personal. So, instead of saying, 'If interested, speak to Bob,' show a photo of Bob with his contact details.
- Communicate grace not guilt. So, instead of saying, 'If no one steps up, it'll have to stop,' say, 'If this interests you, let me know; if not, that's fine.'
- Seek a person not a crowd. So, instead of saying, 'It would be great if you could stay to help at the event later,' say, 'Could three people raise their hands if they can wash-up for half an hour?'
- Consider who needs to know first. So, instead of launching a grand new idea from the front before

you've spoken to anyone else, check with the church leadership and the diary.

- Don't use public platforms for private peeves. Magazines can be prone to this. A church magazine editor is not a law unto themselves. The Bible's call to 'submit to one another out of love' can sometimes mean reining in your opinions or agenda. If you've been entrusted with a public voice, steward it wisely or don't be surprised when it gets muted. Similarly, an unnecessarily controversial notice or display can make destructive ripples in a community. If you see one, feel free to take it down, and talk to people in person instead.

Ask yourself questions first:

- Is it engaging and helpful? Is it kind, necessary, true?
- What am I asking people to do?
- Who is the one person I'm writing this for? Does it answer their questions? Does it answer the question 'what's in it for me?'
- Would it make sense to someone new?
- Have I checked with everyone I need to check with? What could I cut?[61]

Find your team

A communications team with a mix of skills and personalities, probably all volunteers, all committed (we hope) to the same central aim, can achieve the same level of fundamental improvement as a full-time staff member. I've seen it happen. You will need someone with a very good eye to be the person ultimately responsible for any designs that go out. Sometimes someone needs to be willing to say, 'No,' if what's going out won't honour God or reflect the character of the church.

Potential new recruits might be:

- Those most involved in the local community, able to see what you do from the perspective of their neighbours.
- Those passionate about contextual mission.
- Exhibition-goers, photographers, artists, people with graphic design on their walls at home, and opinions about fonts.
- Those who can offer constructive feedback on the magazine, or ideas on Christmas/Easter publicity.
- Anyone who's taken the initiative to improve communication for their ministry, group or club.
- A church leader committed to growing the church.

A team doesn't need to be large. It can start with two or three gathered for prayer. It can include volunteers, those who live out their faith in the workplace and bring that insight into the church.[62]

When working with a communications team I've found these four principles particularly helpful.

1. Share a foundation of grace and truth.
2. Know clearly who is responsible for what.
3. Aim for minimal 'drama'. If you find yourselves in a heated discussion over a poster or misplaced parenthesis it's time for a perspective check.
4. Know when criticism is constructive and when it's mere criticism. There is no excuse for actively discouraging others in a church in the name of 'just being honest', particularly on something as important as communication.

Need volunteers? Pray. Then think whom you would most want to respond if you did a big callout to the whole congregation. Then pray for an opportunity to ask them to pray about it. Volunteer mobilisation and evangelism have this in common: there's nothing, no communication on earth, more powerful than one person speaking honestly to another, powered by prayer.

The very best teams won't be confined to church members. They may include:

- Neighbours who don't go to church.
- People in other local churches. Could you get an hour or two with someone from another local church to share ideas and skills?
- Outside support. There is a list in chapter 4 of great blogs for email support. They're also listed at www.cpo.org.uk/toolkit where you can enquire about a training session. Also look out for conferences and one-off sessions from the denominations and the Evangelical Alliance among others.

In summary

One writer who had vehemently rejected Christianity said that she returned to church 'for the same reason I imagine anyone goes to church, which is that I am compelled and have lost the power to resist'.

The Talking Jesus research in 2015 found that attending church had more impact on people becoming Christians than anything other than growing up in a Christian family. Our welcome, our hospitality and all that we communicate in church, intentionally, sensually and unintentionally, matters enough for you to take action from this book and pass it on.

Talking Jesus concludes with this:

Let's pray for the Church in our nation. We are faced with an enormous challenge but also great opportunities. Simply improving our skills or commitment will not be enough. We need God's intervention. Prayer alongside any action is essential.[63]

4

Toolkit

All these links are also at www.cpo.org.uk/toolkit.

Using your building

- Start here: www.hrballiance.org.uk/resources/help-advice. Church of England churches can use www.parishresources.org.uk.
- Germinate (Arthur Rank Centre) have excellent articles and links, not just for rural churches: bit.ly/2l8n6o4.
- National Churches Trust: bit.ly/2kcTapf
- Churches Conservation Trust guidance and case studies: bit.ly/2jBHX2q; and business plan toolkit: bit.ly/2iXScfO
- Crossing the Threshold: bit.ly/2ke23D5
- Statements of Significance: bit.ly/2k0OYJX
- *How Churches Can Engage with Civic Society* by Roger Sutton, Gather: bit.ly/2jMovmk

Denomination specifics

- Church of England (but relevant to others): www.churchcare.co.uk
- Church of Scotland: bit.ly/2iXpo6W (range of leaflets) and bit.ly/2jjskMc (handbook)
- Church in Wales: bit.ly/2k0bHWx
- Roman Catholic Church in England and Wales: bit.ly/2iNT23m
- The Methodist Church: bit.ly/2jKCvg6
- The Baptist Union: bit.ly/2k0gZS7
- The United Reformed Church suggests you contact your synod's property officer.

Buildings fundraising advice

- The Church of England's Parish Resources: www.parishresources.org.uk/resourcesfor-treasurers/funding, which also has a list of major funders.
- www.cuf.org.uk/near-neighbours/Resources
- The Institute of Fundraising has useful material and videos: www.institute-of-fundraising.org.uk/guidance/introduction-to-fundraising.
- Books by Maggie Durran

Mission-aware church architects

- www.churchbuildingprojects.co.uk
- www.church-architects.co.uk
- www.cplarchitects.co.uk/portfolio.html

On accessibility for disabled people

- www.signsofgod.org.uk: for sign language interpreters
- www.gosign.org.uk: Christian videos with sign language
- www.prospects.org.uk: focus on learning disabilities
- www.torchtrust.org: advice on the visually impaired
- www.disabilityandjesus.org.uk

There is also advice from Church Care (bit.ly/2qFofsI) and Germinate (go to www.germinate.net and search for 'accessibility').

On Christian bookshops and stalls

Get a good feel of the Christian book trade by taking a look at the Facebook pages for 'Christian Resources Together' and 'Christian authors, booksellers and publishers'. You also might want to subscribe to www.christianresourcestogether.co.uk and www.christianbookshopsblog.org.uk. There is practical advice on setting up a bookshop or bookstall here:

- From the bookshops blog: bit.ly/2ksoORi
- From the Good Book Company: bit.ly/2jOmZfg
- From 10ofthose: bit.ly/2kswoLr
- Why encourage people to read books? Go to www.booksforlife.uk.

On coffee shops and cafes

For a thoughtful exploration of cafe, church and coffee, start with this from Fresh Expressions: www.freshexpressions.org.uk/guide/examples/cafe, and link in with www.cafechurch.net.

For fair trade coffee supplies aimed at churches, try www.kingdomcoffee.co.uk.

On church art

- www.acetrust.org
- www.commission4mission.org
- www.christianartists.org.uk
- www.artandsacredplaces.org

Free images

- www.unsplash.com
- commons.wikimedia.org (make sure not to put 'www.' before this link)
- www.flickr.com/creativecommons
- Google: in Google Images, click 'Settings' at the bottom right, then 'Advanced Search'. Under 'Usage rights', choose those 'free to use or share'.
- www.photopin.com
- www.sitebuilderreport.com/stock-up
- www.churchm.ag/unsplashalternatives
- www.morguefile.com

Photo guidelines

- A visual overview of church design layout can be found in the free download linked to the Grove booklet 'Publicity and the Local Church' by Nicola David: bit.ly/GrovePublicity.

Advice and tools to create your own images:

- pablo.buffer.com (make sure not to put 'www.' before this link)
- spark.adobe.com (make sure not to put 'www.' before this link)
- www.canva.com

Church logos

- www.cmsucks.us/n1
- www.churchlogogallery.com
- www.outreach.com/Church-Logos

Design brief questions

Answer these before commissioning a designer:

1. What is the goal of your project, in no more than two sentences?
2. Who is your target audience (for example, age, gender, worldview, location)?
3. Do you want them to do something specific as a result of the project (e.g. check a website)?
4. Do you have specific format requirements?
5. Where do you expect this to be seen?
6. How do you want people to feel when they see this?
7. Does it need to sit alongside or appear to be linked with any other design?
8. Do you have any samples of inspiration? Have you seen anything you'd like to build on?
9. Are there brand guidelines or an established look and feel that needs to be followed?
10. Can you nominate an individual to be responsible?

Data protection and church copyright

London Diocese's parish communications toolkit has up-to-date sections on copyright and on data: bitly.com/ParishCommsToolkit.

On data protection, churches are subject to the rules set out by www.ico.gov.uk. A helpful briefing for churches is at bitly.com/StewardshipData.

For advice on music, lyrics and video, contact CCLI (01323 436100; www.ccli.com).

Making church videos

- Free training: www.prochurchtools.com/church-video-series
- 'Church video production for newbies': bit.ly/2kDWOMt
- 'The Best Royalty Free Production Music Sites': bit.ly/2jOEGLI

Church communications blogs

- www.churchmarketingsucks.com
- www.churchm.ag
- www.prochurchtools.com

- www.churchtrain.uk
- www.premierdigital.org.uk

More at www.cpo.org.uk/toolkit

Church online administration providers

- www.churchbox.co.uk
- www.churchbuilder.co.uk
- www.churchapp.co.uk
- www.churchinsight.com
- www.iknowchurch.co.uk
- GoogleDocs and Dropbox are often also used by churches.
- Advice on SMS providers at www.cpo.org.uk/toolkit

Proofreading checklist

- Is the basic information clear and accurate?
- Are the names spelled correctly?
- Is it relevant for the audience? Is the tone right?
- Is it consistent in its terminology?

For more help on church magazines, have a free trial at www.parishpump.co.uk.

UK church digital signage specialists

- www.apicommunications.co.uk
- www.a-a.uk.com
- www.spectra-displays.co.uk

You can also receive help from Christian technical consultancies, such as www.isidore.co.uk, or help with sound and lighting from Christian church specialists, such as www.crystalclearaudio.co.uk.

Song lyric/worship presentation software

Whatever you do, don't use PowerPoint. There are loads of tools that already have thousands of songs with the correct words ready to go. You need a copyright licence from CCLI. Then you can also purchase a licence for software that will display songs, and also produce music and chord sheets. Song Select is a song library resource from CCLI designed for the UK which enables you search by keywords, writer, lyric and theme, and transpose to the right key signature. Start here: www.churches.uk.ccli.com/2016/01/whats-with-all-the-software. Here are some reviews of popular tools:

- bit.ly/2kfGOzL on EasyWorship, ProPresenter and Media Shout; bit.ly/2kfCd0k focusing on Power Music and Zionworx; bit.ly/2kGRatc focusing on OpenLP, OpenSong, FreeWorship
- bit.ly/2lbZEpL: a list of Song Select API partners

Videos in services

- www.gochattervideos.com
- www.worshiphousemedia.com
- www.sermonspice.com
- www.videosforyouth.com
- www.lifechurch.tv
- www.creationswap.com
- www.godtube.com
- www.truetube.co.uk.

To build a picture of the UK church

- www.greatcommission.co.uk from the Evangelical Alliance
- *Talking Jesus*: www.talkingjesus.org
- Bob Jackson, *What Makes Churches Grow?* (Church House Publishing, 2015)

To build a picture of your locality

- The Centre for Theology & Community has a list of sources to map, for example, poverty or religious affiliation, with questions for churches to use: bit.ly/2l494XE.
- Census summaries from www.neighbourhood.statistics.gov.uk/dissemination, or the incredible www.datashine.org.uk.
- A free trial of Acorn (www.acorn.caci.co.uk) will describe your neighbours down to where they're likely to shop.
- If you're brave enough to use a questionnaire to find out what people think of your church, sample questions might include:
  - How long have you lived in the area? What local services do you use?
  - What do you think are some of the issues locally?
  - Have you ever connected with [name of church] in any way? Have you visited the church hall or equivalent?
  - Did you know that the church offers…? Would you find it useful to be notified of future courses/events?
  - Would you like prayer?

Notes

1   Henri Nouwen, *Reaching Out* (Bantam Doubleday Dell, 2000), p. 71.
2   Sandra Millar, *Stepping into the Unknown*, bit.ly/2iO0lH9.
3   Don Draper, *Mad Men*, 'The Wheel' (2007).
4   Kem Meyer, *Less Chaos. Less Noise* (Less Chaos. Less Noise, 2016), p. 237.
5   From the National Literacy Trust, bit.ly/2jjSSNx.
6   Cleve Persinger, *Dangerous: A go-to guide for church communication* (CreateSpace Independent Publishing Platform, 2013), p. 2.
7   www.nationalchurchestrust.org/toilets.
8   'Report from the Archbishops' Evangelism Task Group' (General Synod, 2016), p. 36, bit.ly/2kd2Ss1.
9   National Churches Trust, *The National Churches Trust Survey*, 2011, bit.ly/2iOu4Ba.
10 1 Peter 4:7–11.
11 Steve Aisthorpe, *The Invisible Church* (St Andrew Press, 2016), p. 103.
12 Persinger, *Dangerous*, p. 19.
13 Meyer, *Less Chaos*, p. 44.
14 www.chuckscoggins.com/blog/2014/10/13/how-to-decide.
15 Try 24-7prayer.com, thykingdomcome.global, messychurch.org.uk/tags/prayer or the many ideas at www.flamecreativekids.blogspot.co.uk.

16   Bob Jackson, *What Makes Churches Grow?* (Church
     House Publishing, 2015), p. 7.

17   Youthscape, *Losing Heart*, December 2016,
     bit.ly/2jRfxQz.

18   Olwyn Mark, *Passing on Faith* (Theos, 2016),
     bit.ly/2jPgi1q. For helpful reflections from
     Ali Campbell on these research reports, see
     bit.ly/2kek4Bt.

19   Phoebe Hill, 'Why the Church Doesn't Have to Lose
     a Generation of Young People', *Christian Today*,
     December 2016, bit.ly/2iOx1le.

20   bit.ly/2kcX5Tg.

21   Church Support Hub: www.churchsupporthub.
     org. School visit advice from SU: bit.ly/2nmo3MP.
     Tourist advice links from CVTA (www.cvta.org.uk)
     and Church Care (bit.ly/2iYkNkU).

22   Blog advice on QR codes from Churches Alive
     Online: bit.ly/2keraFQ and piota.co.uk.

23   There are examples at www.christianityandculture.
     org.uk/partnerships.

24   Eyam Parish Church, www.eyam-church.org.

25   Traidcraft and Kingdom Coffee are good sources.

26   Revd Elaine Richardson, 'Welcoming the homeless
     and offering hospitality to the Herne community',
     Outlook (Diocese of Canterbury, Spring 2012), p. 15,
     bit.ly/2k6881F.

27   For starters, try the 'Tracts & Outreach' section at
     www.cpo.org.uk, Scripture Union, the Good Book
     Company, the Bible Society and Philo Trust.

28 Church Army, 'Seeing the Bigger Picture: Four reports on fresh expressions in the Church of England', bit.ly/2kgLp5w.

29 Richard Reising, *Church Marketing 101* (Baker, 2006), p. 35.

30 Evangelical Alliance, Church of England and Hope Together, *Talking Jesus: Perceptions of Jesus, Christians and evangelism in England* (2015).

31 Barna Group, *What millennials want when they visit church*, March 2015, bit.ly/2kgR2As.

32 Haydn Shaw, *Generational IQ* (Tyndale House Publishers, 2015), p. 2017. More information at www.christianityisnotdying.com.

33 Martyn Payne, *Messy Togetherness: Being intergenerational in Messy Church* (BRF, 2016).

34 Church of England Education Office, *Rooted in the Church: Summary report*, November 2016, bit.ly/2phpIkb.

35 Nicola James, *Publicity and the Local Church* (Grove Books, 2007), p. 8.

36 www.parishofchingford.org.uk.

37 Laura Bennett, *Dangerous: A go-to guide for church communication* (CreateSpace Independent Publishing Platform, 2013), p. 32.

38 Attributed to Samuel Smiles, *Happy Homes and the Hearts that Make Them* (U.S. Publishing House, 1883).

39 bit.ly/2kCEW2b and www.bbc.in/2kI0IoD.

40 There are great ideas at www.freshworship.org and

on Jonny Baker's blog, bit.ly/2k6hgn1.

41 There's a guide at www.cpo.org.uk.

42 Simon Jenkins, *England's Cathedrals* (Little, Brown 2016), p. xxv.

43 Matthew Hall, '50 Things to Do in a Church', Diocese of London, August 2016, bit.ly/2kgOKle.

44 *National Churches Trust Survey.*

45 National Churches Trust, *Attitudes to Church Buildings: findings of an opinion poll commissioned by the National Churches Trust—December 2014*, bit.ly/2kHNJDl; also *National Churches Trust Survey*, p. 22.

46 Find out more at www.champing.co.uk.

47 From *Crossing the Threshold* (Diocese of Hereford, 2013): bit.ly/2kh3gZM.

48 For a list of where to go by denomination see p. 82.

49 www.church-textiles.co.uk

50 Use the links listed in chapter 4.

51 Matthew Hall, 'New-Monastic living on an ancient pathway', Diocese of London, May 2014, bit.ly/2kgWGmc.

52 Many people have found www.worshipcentral.org and www.missionworship.com helpful.

53 Ben Blackwell, Kate Bruce and Peter Phillips, *The View from the Pew: a pilot research project on the reception of preaching within the contemporary church* (University of Durham, 2009), p. 7.

54 Explained fully in Robert Poynton, *Do/Improvise* (The Do Book Company, 2012), p. 47.

55 www.christian-research.org/reports/what-do-you-want-from-a-sermon.

56 www.preachweb.org.

57 For free images, see page 85.

58 I liked this comment on an internet forum: 'It's quite a moving experience, not to be staring at each other, but to face forward as one crew of one battleship, looking toward the captain who is leading from the bow: Christ…', bit.ly/2jGuZ5u.

59 Whichever song lyric software you use—see page 89—remember that clever fonts and moving pictures in the background can easily detract from, rather than enhance, the worship. Less is more!

60 Try www.gochattervideos.com; www.worshiphousemedia.com; www.sermonspice.com; www.videosforyouth.com; www.lifechurch.tv; www.creationswap.com; www.godtube.com.

61 Abbreviated from Meyer, *Less Chaos*, p. 327.

62 For more on this, see resources from the London Institute of Contemporary Christianity, such as the course 'Life on the Frontline', www.licc.org.uk.

63 *Talking Jesus*, p. 25.